How Cyber Security Can Protect Your Business

A guide for all stakeholders

How Cyber Security Can Protect Your Business

A guide for all stakeholders

CHRISTOPHER WRIGHT

IT Governance Publishing

Every possible effort has been made to ensure that the information contained in this book is accurate at the time of going to press, and the publisher and the author cannot accept responsibility for any errors or omissions, however caused. Any opinions expressed in this book are those of the author, not the publisher. Websites identified are for reference only, not endorsement, and any website visits are at the reader's own risk. No responsibility for loss or damage occasioned to any person acting, or refraining from action, as a result of the material in this publication can be accepted by the publisher or the author.

Apart from any fair dealing for the purposes of research or private study, or criticism or review, as permitted under the Copyright, Designs and Patents Act 1988, this publication may only be reproduced, stored or transmitted, in any form, or by any means, with the prior permission in writing of the publisher or, in the case of reprographic reproduction, in accordance with the terms of licences issued by the Copyright Licensing Agency. Enquiries concerning reproduction outside those terms should be sent to the publisher at the following address:

IT Governance Publishing Ltd
Unit 3, Clive Court
Bartholomew's Walk
Cambridgeshire Business Park
Ely, Cambridgeshire
CB7 4EA
United Kingdom
www.itgovernancepublishing.co.uk

The author has asserted the rights of the author under the Copyright, Designs and Patents Act, 1988, to be identified as the author of this work.

First published in the United Kingdom in 2019 by IT Governance Publishing.

ISBN 978-1-78778-195-5

FOREWORD

I was in the audience at an ISACA® conference in Manchester when Chris delivered a lecture on information security audits. It was pretty clear that, with almost four decades' experience, he had mastery of the subject. Despite the fact the room was full of seasoned audit professionals, he delivered his lecture in simple language that you did not have to be an information security audit professional to understand. At the end, he spoke about his new book *How Cyber Security Can Protect Your Business – A guide for all stakeholders* and how he wanted to demystify cyber.

When he approached me to review the book and write a foreword, little did he know that I was an apostle of the title, and actually own the *cybergrc.uk* domain to promote cyber security good practice. Nearly every day, I sit down with CEOs, CISOs, CROs and IT directors to discuss their business' cyber security audit requirements, assess their operational resilience by testing the effectiveness and adequacy of their administrative and technical controls, and make recommendations for improvements where opportunities are found.

This book is cleverly written to appeal to all audiences irrespective of their background. It dissects cyber security, covering everything that a professional, non-professional or organisation needs to know to operate a safe cyber environment. It recognises the importance of having a C-level sponsor in an organisation to promote cyber security investment, and makes clear that operating in a safe environment is everybody's business, not just IT professionals'. The clarity around cyber governance, risk management and compliance cannot be overemphasised. Each chapter discusses the components of the cyber audit review lifecycle, highlighting the risk control matrix approach to assessing risks, testing controls and signalling a pathway to providing assurance for stakeholders.

This book is an ideal guide for individuals wanting to start a career in cyber security audit and advisory, and a practical reference source for experienced auditors, with the author summarising his decades of experience to create a soft landing for others who wish to take off or progress from where he is taking a bow.

Yours cyberly,

Yinka Akingbehin

PREFACE

'Cyber' is a word we use all the time. But what does it mean? What are the implications for us as directors and general managers? Or as IT security managers and auditors?

'Cyber' is thought to derive from the older term 'cybernetics' – based on electronic/mechanical control systems and the degree to which man-made and human worlds interact. Cybernetics is derived from the Greek word 'kubernan' – to steer or control. Kubernan is derived from the Greek word 'kubernetetes' – or steersman. So, we can think of cyber as the balance of control between humans and computers. It is now usually understood to cover most things computer/IT/Internet of Things (IoT) related.

This 'control' aspect is often overlooked. One of the reasons for this has been technical deafness on the part of business – they hear the words but zone out until the concepts of profit or loss/cost reduction are mentioned, and then tend to focus just on those. IT professionals have been more interested in bits and bytes and other exciting techie stuff. One of the exciting aspects of cyber is that these two worlds of business and technology management have started to merge. Partly because of a growing awareness of the threats facing cyber reliance, and partly as a response to increased pressure from regulators, the media and other agencies. What both tribes now need is a go-between.

It's about balance: how do we continue to safely and confidently enjoy the benefits of our modern life – instant communication, and the ability to order goods and services whenever and wherever we want, having checked our bank balances and socially networked all of our friends to brag about our purchases.

The aim of governance, risk and compliance (GRC), according to *SAP GRC for Dummies*, is to:

Efficiently put policies and controls in place to address all
its compliance obligations while at the same time gathering
information that helps proactively run the business.[1]

However, GRC is more than that. It is not just about ensuring
compliance obligations are met, but also about providing
assurance that significant risks that could impact the future
viability and profitability of the organisation have been
addressed. Increasingly this includes the reliance on information
and cyber activity.

The preceding definition does partly explain why IT security
professionals are sometimes opposed to GRC. It is seen as an
overhead that does not provide business benefit and can get in
the way of what they are trying to achieve. The irony is that this
is exactly how project managers, IT service providers, and other
information/IT managers see IT security/cyber management.
They consider them as blockers rather than enablers. GRC
should be seen as an opportunity to promote good cyber
governance throughout an organisation in order to provide an
effective foundation for cyber security.

The purpose of this book is therefore to provide an effective and
efficient framework for cyber GRC. Like all frameworks, it will
need to be adapted for each organisation to meet their own risk
appetite and synchronise with their GRC policies, processes and
tools. The book explains what is meant by GRC, how it applies
to cyber and what is required to implement effective cyber GRC.
Its aim is to guide managers and executives without resorting to
'cyber-babble'; any feedback on whether it achieves this is
welcome. The book will be of interest to non-cyber specialists,
including non-executive directors, who may be required to
review cyber arrangements. For cyber specialists, it provides an
approach for explaining cyber issues in non-jargonistic,
business-based language.

---

[1] Denise Vu Broady and Holly A Roland, *SAP GRC for Dummies!*,
Dummies, 2008.

ABOUT THE AUTHOR

A qualified accountant, certified information systems auditor and certified ScrumMaster, Chris has more than 35 years' experience providing IT security advisory and audit/risk management services. He worked for 16 years at KPMG where he managed several major information security audit and risk assignments, including reviews of project risks and business controls. He was head of information risk training in the UK and ran training courses overseas, including India and throughout mainland Europe. Chris has worked in a wide range of industry sectors, including oil and gas, public sector, aviation and travel. These assignments included cyber, GRC implementation and audit, and the implementation of cyber-based projects.

For the past 12 years he has been an independent consultant specialising in financial, Sarbanes-Oxley Act (SOX) and operational controls for major ERP implementations.

Chris is an international speaker and trainer on Agile audit and governance issues, and has written four other titles for IT Governance Publishing: *Agile Governance and Audit* (2014), *Reviewing IT in Due Diligence* (2015), *Fundamentals of Information Risk Management Auditing* (2016) and *Fundamentals of Assurance for Lean Projects* (2017).

Chris has also contributed to publications from professional working groups on third-party compliance and management and Agile project assurance.

He also implemented a GRC system for cyber/IT security management at a major customer services organisation. This included:

- Developing IT/cyber security policies;
- Implementing compliance processes and tools;
- Designing and implementing board reporting for cyber compliance; and
- Designing, testing and implementing cyber SOX controls frameworks.

He is also a speaker and technical reviewer, and seeks to bridge the gap between general and cyber management to achieve effective governance, risk management and compliance within organisations.

ACKNOWLEDGEMENTS

I would like to thank those who assisted in the production of this book: Sophie, Nicky and Vicki at ITGP, Jonathan Todd at ITG, Chris Evans for his review of my manuscript, and my long-term friends Scott Nichols, John Jones, Mike Hughes and Yinka Akingbehin for their valuable feedback.

Last but by no means least, my wife, Amanda, for her patience, feedback and support.

CONTENTS

Contents

CHAPTER 1: INTRODUCTION TO CYBER SECURITY GRC

Background to GRC

Governance. Risk. Compliance (or 'Control'). Simple words – but they encompass so much. They cover the steps taken by organisations to ensure they act ethically, legally and with integrity, and can effectively and efficiently handle risks (or other uncertainties) in achieving their business goals or other objectives.

GRC was first defined by Scott Mitchell, OCEG, in 2007 as:

> the integrated collection of capabilities that enable an organization to reliably achieve objectives, address uncertainty and act with integrity.[2]

Governance is the ability to ensure that the organisation achieves its goals and objectives. It includes policies and processes led by senior management and the board to provide overall control of their activities. Ultimately, they are accountable for the financial health and legal compliance of the organisation – sometimes at risk of criminal proceedings. Governance also includes providing the ethics and tone of the organisation, as well as the structures and policies within which it operates.

Risk management is the ability to confidently act in a world of uncertainty: the process by which the organisation identifies, assesses and reviews the risks it faces in performing its operations. It also considers controls for these risks and ensures that adequate mitigations are in place (i.e. controls, insurance or risk acceptance).

Compliance, the ability to act with ethical integrity, is the adherence to applicable laws and regulations, as well as to the company's own policies and procedures.

---

[2] _www.oceg.org/about/what-is-grc/_.

The basic principles of GRC apply to all organisations regardless of size. However, the processes, people, information and technology used to achieve good GRC vary considerably between organisations depending mainly on their size and areas of activity. For example, whereas a large banking organisation will face complex governance issues (need for experienced and knowledgeable board members, risk management and compliance issues), and their compliance requirements will include financial regulations and anti-money laundering, a small corner café is likely to be owned and governed by a small number of people but needs to comply with food hygiene and other relevant regulations.

GRC can be seen as an overhead – some might say GRC is an additional activity that does not directly add to the success or financial health of the organisation. Where GRC activity is not focused or co-ordinated, there can be redundant activities that neither provide business benefit nor strengthen the organisation's governance, risk management or compliance. The aim is to simplify and manage the GRC process in such a way that it enables the organisation to fulfil its objectives, for example by providing the capability to enter new markets where the risk profile or compliance requirements are different to those for the rest of the organisation. This may involve embedding the risk management and compliance processes in normal business activities while automatically producing the key performance indicators (KPIs) and other reporting required by the main stakeholders for their governance activities. The main consideration is to provide a robust approach to handling the challenges of uncertainty and the risk of loss of reputation or customers, and even in some cases the risk of prison! Another benefit can be that when mergers and acquisitions take place, the target company can more easily be integrated into the acquiring organisation's GRC framework.

GRC activities are often spread across organisations, including board secretariat, internal audit, compliance teams and risk teams in legal, finance, IT and HR, as well as within normal business operations. This can lead to conflicting activities across the different silos. There can also be inconsistencies in the level and type of risk being addressed – risks important at local/departmental levels may be minute when compared to those of the organisation as a whole. Also, in large, complex organisations these activities may be replicated across the different constituent entities. In these cases there can therefore be duplications of activities and gaps in coverage. Enterprise governance, risk and compliance (EGRC) seeks to provide a consistent, integrated approach to GRC across the organisation to reduce these duplications and potential duplications. It also provides a framework of policies, tools, processes and information reporting to simplify the activity and provide consistency.

The three lines of defence model

To provide governance of the risk management process itself, many organisations use the three lines of defence model[3] to explain their approach to managing risk. This model helps to assign specific risk management roles and responsibilities/duties, and to define the boundaries between them. The model is illustrated in Table 1.

Table 1: Summary of the Three Lines of Defence Model

Line	Usually performed by	Typical activities
First line – operational management control	Business functions	• Embedded risk management. • Direct contact with risks.

---

[3] *IIA Position Paper* "The Three Lines of Defense in Effective Risk Management and Control", OECG.

		• Highlight control failures/unexpected events. • Remediate to address process/control deficiencies.
Second line – risk control and compliance oversight	Risk committees Risk functions (e.g. CISO)	• Provide frameworks and support implementation of relevant policies and procedures. • Help build/monitor first line. • Develop processes and controls to manage risks and issues. • Review and update registers and responses to risks faced. • Operate self-certification/compliance processes.
Third line – independent assurance	Audit and the board	• Provide independent review and reporting of the organisation's

		response to risk, including first two lines.

The model can be applied to organisations of any size or complexity – the aim is to provide a risk management framework that is effective (fit for purpose), efficient (limited impact on normal, legitimate operations) and economic (costs not excessive given the level of risk or compliance needs). The boundaries between the lines may also vary. If this model is used, it is important that the three lines have been defined within the organisation, including how the different lines should interact, including in the sharing of findings and information about risks/incidents and issues. A risk is something that could happen; an issue is something that has happened.

Within the context of cyber, the three lines could be considered as follows:

1. Operational management, SEC OPS functions Managed Security Services Provider (MSSP), Third party suppliers and service providers.

2. CISO and other compliance/review functions (in part this may be incorporated into non-cyber activities, e.g. data compliance).

3. Qualified IT auditors/ISO audits.

For cyber (as with health and safety), staff should be considered the first line of defence. For example, while operational management may ensure that anti-malware is installed and updated, the end user may still compromise security by clicking a phishing link or visiting an inappropriate site. All users need to be educated on cyber risks and made aware of the risks and consequences both to them as individuals and to the organisation as a whole. This awareness could have benefits for their personal lives as well.

Another concern is that the model can be seen as silo based. To work effectively, the different defence lines need to be integrated, e.g. to reduce the risk of a blame culture between the lines if and when a breach occurs.

What is the relevance of GRC to cyber?

We live in a digital cyber-based world – we use IT to communicate with friends and family, purchase goods and services, and do our banking, to name just a few activities. Cyber security could be defined as:

> Measures to prevent or detect electronic attempts of theft or damage to your data and IT assets.

Cyber is not very different from any other risk impacting a business. It can affect an organisation's reputation, compliance (including data privacy and specific cyber compliance) and financial well-being. Cyber is not just an IT issue – it impacts the whole way that you do business and organisational administration.

Cyber is not exempt from GRC. We need to ensure that cyber-based security activities are in line with all other GRC activities of the organisation and are subject to similar governance and control. Indeed, given the threats and risks specific to cyber, it could be argued that GRC is even more important.

If we consider this from the cyber criminal's perspective, they may create a user story as follows:

> "As a ne'er-do-well, I want to access and change your data and information/deny you access to your systems and data so that I can meet my own evil agenda by damaging your reputation and/or extort a ransom or other financial reward. To achieve this, I will target organisations that have little or no overall control of cyber. They:
>
> - Employ badly trained users who are gullible to threats;
>
> - Have risk management processes that are not working (don't update security tools such as anti-malware, no effective password management, etc.); and

- Fail to comply with laws/regulations/best-practice cyber hygiene."

Your job as a director, manager or cyber security specialist is to stop them. One way to do this is to ensure that your organisation has effective cyber GRC. We will explore how to achieve this in the following chapters.

It is also important to remember that the impact of a cyber incident can go well beyond the immediate costs. We have seen companies across the globe go into receivership following a cyber attack, particularly where there has been a breach of personal data. This can be due to loss of reputation/customers and/or potentially massive regulatory fines.

We will now consider how good GRC can help reduce these risks.

CHAPTER 2: CYBER SECURITY GOVERNANCE

*"Boards are pivotal in improving the cyber security of
their organisations."*

NCSC Cyber Security Toolkit for Boards

Introduction and overview

Good control requires good corporate governance from the top
(directors and executive management). Top management should
ensure that the organisation is well structured and managed with
strong policies and a strong ethos. Governance forms the
foundation on which other controls and risk mitigations can be
built. For example, controls will only be effective if there is the
culture to ensure that they are adhered to and that anyone
breaking these rules will be held to account and treated
accordingly. Ultimately, those who hold governance
accountability will be held responsible for all failures regardless
of where they occur.

These corporate governance, 'entity-level controls' are
pervasive throughout the organisation, including information
and cyber activities. They set the culture and tone for the
organisation to operate. They should not, however, interfere
with day-to-day operations, except where such activities could
put the organisation at financial, legal/fiscal or reputational risk.
The aim of good governance is shown in Figure 1.

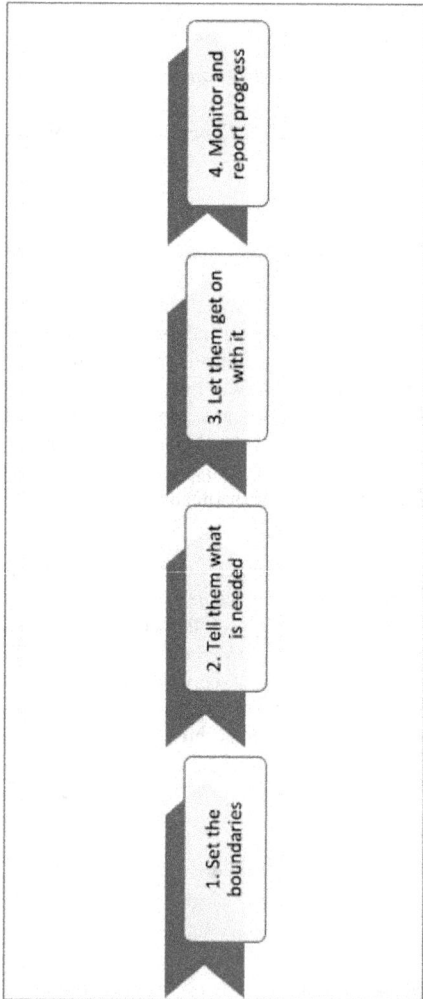

Figure 1: Governance flow

Even small organisations are at increased risk from cyber criminals as they can often be used as a weak starting point to target other organisations in the same supply chain. A key part of cyber criminals' approach is to 'case the joint' or investigate their targets – this will include reading press releases about the awards of new contracts and the details of these customers and suppliers. Therefore, all directors owe a duty of care, not only to their own organisation's stakeholders but also to those of key business partners.

Directors and senior staff may be targeted in the same way, as cyber criminals search social media, etc. to gather information they can use when impersonating them via email or another form of contact. Directors must be made aware of the need to manage their personal social media presence securely.

Very few directors are cyber security specialists. But all directors need to have a basic understanding and awareness of cyber security based on jargon-free principles. To help with this, we could express governance as a user story from the Director's perspective:

As a director I want assurance, in concise, understandable language, that we have:

- Adequate management of cyber risks and threats

- Been made aware of significant attacks and near misses, and advised of actions to prevent re-occurrence

- Been made aware of security arrangements for our significant third parties including any significant attacks

- Used our investment in cyber security effectively and efficiently

So that we reduce the impact and likelihood of loss of reputation, large fines, and other consequences of data breaches and loss of ability to do cyber business through cyber risk.

Acceptance criteria

To achieve this, I will need the Chief Information Security Officer (CISO) to provide regular, concise and easy-to-understand reports of:

1. The threat landscape relevant to our business;

2. Whether we have an organisational culture that is aware of these threats and acts appropriately;

3. Progress we are making to reduce the risk (e.g. anti-malware deployment, attack management, user awareness, phishing programme, recent audit results);

4. Attacks/breaches and how we have responded; and

5. Latest reviews of IT security policies and other security communications.

This approach helps to explain the requirements and provides focus for both boards of directors and those who report to them.

In the event of a breach or incident, any investigating regulators, such as the Information Commissioner's Office (ICO) in the UK and the SEC if the company is US listed, will want to examine the cyber governance in place. They may consider:

- The overall GRC framework;

- Culture and awareness;

- Threat and risk awareness;

- Cyber risk management; and

- Preparation for and response to attack.

They will look for evidence of these activities, including board reports, meeting minutes and follow-up actions.

Culture and awareness

All staff need awareness of cyber security and how it impacts
their role and duties. It should not be just an issue for cyber
security specialists, but instead form part of the organisation's
overall hygiene – much the same as health and safety, for
example. Anyone who uses IT (and most will) is a key risk – but
also a control to prevent cyber attacks. However, this 'human
firewall' will only be effective if users are made aware of their
cyber security responsibilities, given the tools to operate safely
and securely (e.g. installed anti-malware), and motivated to act
appropriately, including a willingness to report cyber risks
and/or attacks immediately and effectively. Organisations must
ensure that it is easier for staff to perform the right behaviours
than the wrong ones. Motivation also includes ensuring that
these correct behaviours are recognised, and giving positive
feedback. Failure to provide a response, for example after the
reporting of an attempted phishing email, may lead to the
individual not reporting future incidents.

Good cultural change also relies on directors leading by
example. It is inappropriate for directors to be a special case and
excluded from the controls applied to everyone else, such as
being allowed to use their own unsecured IT devices. Where
directors encounter a problem with a policy or procedure, this is
the same for all users in the organisation – the emphasis should
be on finding a better way to achieve the objective rather than
allowing an exception or waiver for directors (who may be at
higher risk of a cyber attack).

The message needs to be re-enforced at every opportunity –
cyber security is not just for the annual security campaign. Better
cyber security will benefit all users – not only in their work but
also personally as they will be more aware of scams such as
approaches from bogus banks or broadband service providers.

The board should receive regular reports on any campaigns and
the level of user awareness of cyber risks and threats. This helps
give an indication of the cyber security health of the
organisation. Cyber ratings are publicly available indicators, like
credit ratings but based on cyber hygiene indicators, that can also

indicate an organisation's resilience, and can be tracked over time.

Threat and risk awareness

The board needs to ensure that there are effective and efficient processes in place to understand the cyber threats faced by their organisation, based upon:

- The type of operation and any imminent changes;

- The extent of digital and cyber activity;

- Geographies they operate in;

- Previous cyber issues;

- Awareness of general and specific threats and vulnerabilities; and

- Vulnerabilities due to technologies used (e.g. reliance on outdated technology that can

- not be patched for known weaknesses).

There are several publicly available and private service providers that provide regular updates on the specific emerging threat landscape. Where there is cyber insurance in place, the insurer may also provide cyber intelligence reporting. The board should receive regular reports summarising the information provided and be informed of the effectiveness, cost and efficiency of the services provided.

Risk management

Directors need to ensure that there are processes and procedures for risk management and that these are operating effectively. This should include regular reporting of any known control weaknesses, the remediation actions taken and progress in resolving any high-risk areas. Where risks cannot be mitigated or controlled, it may be necessary to implement cyber insurance. The board may be required to provide evidence of this review as part of the cyber insurance cover for their organisation. Cyber risks are usually not covered by traditional policies for the organisation's liability/professional indemnity. Specific policies for cyber provide additional cover for responding to incidents or data breaches.

Risk management processes and specific cyber risks will be considered in subsequent chapters.

Responding to cyber incidents

The board needs to ensure that there is an effective plan in place to deal with a cyber attack, and that it has been tested, communicated and rehearsed. This may include, for example, the use of outside support agencies such as ransomware negotiators, and identifying processes and procedures for escalation to the board and regulators. The plan should include communication arrangements to third parties and the media, detailing the communication chains and the training key staff should receive in media management. The plan should be reviewed and approved annually by the board, with additional reviews following a major cyber incident.

Cyber SOX

The Sarbanes-Oxley Act is legislation specific to companies registered on the US Stock Exchange (similar legislation exists in Japan for Japanese companies). It was introduced following financial reporting scandals to provide reassurance to markets and investors that financial reporting could be relied upon to make investment decisions. Organisations are required to implement controls to ensure the accuracy and completeness of financial reports, both of which are reviewed independently by the auditors as part of their annual review processes. From 2018, additional requirements were introduced for cyber. These require quarterly reporting to enable investors to make decisions based on the organisation's cyber risk management and its response to any recent attacks. There is also emphasis on ensuring that those involved in responding to an incident do not use their 'insider knowledge' to personally benefit via their share dealings.

Summary: key cyber security questions for directors to ask

Cyber security specialists may need to provide guidance on the questions that directors should be asking. Good cyber managers should be able to answer the following questions immediately.

Culture and awareness

- How aware are staff of the risks we face and the controls they need to operate?

- What is the process for reviewing, updating and approving IT and cyber security policies?

- How are the cyber security policies, procedures and controls publicised and enforced?

- What can the board do to improve the cyber awareness culture? (E.g. reward good cyber behaviour, be seen to lead by example.)

Threat/risk awareness and assessment

- How have we identified the cyber threats relevant to our organisation?

- How and when is this process reviewed?

- How do we gather intelligence to monitor the changing threat landscape?

- How is the board informed of these threats and risks?

- What can the board do to improve awareness of risks and threats?

Response to cyber incidents

- What plans are in place to respond to a cyber incident or data breach?

- Is there an effective media management process including training?

- When were these most recently reviewed and tested?

- Have lessons learned sessions been held for all major incidents and breaches? Has the plan been updated accordingly?

Risk management

- What are the processes and procedures for assessing the risks and controls for cyber?

- Have these been recently reviewed?

- What cyber-insurance cover is in place?

- How is the board notified of any known weaknesses and approved exceptions to controls?

- Who is responsible for providing regular reporting on cyber risk management to the board?

Which leads us to the next chapter.

CHAPTER 3: CYBER SECURITY RISK MANAGEMENT

> Disturb us, Lord …
> Because we have dreamed too little,
> When we arrived safely
> Because we sailed too close to the shore.
>
> Prayer often attributed to Sir Francis Drake

Introduction and overview

We all take risks every day. Life is a risky business. But without risk there is no progress. The same applies to organisations in the cyber world: there are risks of hacking, fraud, state interference and identity theft. But these have to be matched against risks of not doing business via cyber (e.g. failure to win new customers or reduce costs). The risks are great but so are the potential rewards: competitive advantage, reduction in costs, increased awareness of your products and services via social media, to name but a few. These risks can be managed in the same way you manage the daily risk of driving – by controls (ensuring your car is roadworthy and that you wear a seat belt, and having it serviced by a qualified technician), by following the rules (speed limits) and by insuring against the unknown risks that you cannot prevent. Every organisation needs to have a process for managing cyber risks.

The process and terminology will vary between organisations, but the basic steps are likely to be as shown in Figure 2. Wherever possible, they should also be followed for cyber. They will help ensure that risks are stated in a format and style that business managers and executives can relate to.

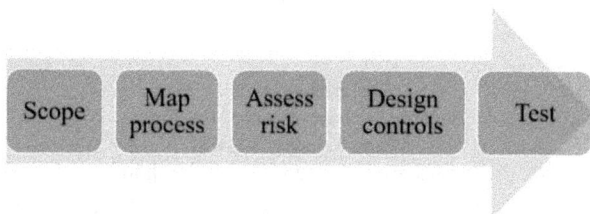

Figure 2: Risk management process

The objective, key activities and deliverables for each of these steps is described below. We will also consider how the risk management process can be made more agile.

Risk management scoping

When undertaking a risk management review, it is important to ensure that the scope is understood and agreed so that there are no gaps or duplication of effort.

For cyber, we need to ensure that all risk assessments are conducted to the same level of detail, based upon the risk appetite of the organisation, otherwise:

- Controls may be defined at too fine a level of detail, leading to extra effort with little or no reduction in the risk profile; or

- Risks identified as strategic for the organisation may not be covered adequately. For example, strategic risks relating to sensitive geographic operating locations or trading in restricted parts of the world could have cyber implications that need to be considered.

The main activities will be:

- Identifying relevant strategic risks, based on the enterprise risk strategy and level of risk appetite determined by the key stakeholders;

- Agreeing the processes, technology and locations in scope, and whether to include activities of third parties/the supply chain;

- Identifying any known incidents or risks specific to the review;

- Identifying all stakeholders, people, procedures and technology to be included in the review; and

- Determining the legal and other regulations that must be considered during the review.

The deliverable from the scoping exercise, which may be from a workshop or a series of meetings, will be an agreed scope, a high-level plan and background notes. To reduce the risk of scope creep or change during the exercise, this documentation should be reviewed and approved by all key stakeholders before the work starts.

Process and control mapping

Documenting the process and related controls helps confirm understanding and ensure that the controls are located at the point of risks so that any errors or attacks can be identified effectively and efficiently. If controls are located too far into the process, this can lead to additional, unnecessary corrective work. The documentation does not need to be too detailed – the aim is to consider the end-to-end process and identify key inputs, outputs and sub-processes. Often this documentation can be prepared following interviews, reviews of existing documentation, and workshops. The key step is to walk through the process and controls wherever possible to confirm understanding and identify any potential variations. For example, if we were looking at access controls for a new cyber application, we may consider whether they will work the same way for all devices/platforms. This step can also ensure that the documentation is accurate and easy to follow, and can highlight where additional documentation may be required to help users undertake key steps.

Output from this phase will be process maps and documentation. The format and tools used to generate these vary between organisations.

Risk assessment

A risk assessment can now be performed to identify key weak points in the process where error or attack could occur. This may also include considering known vulnerabilities for the technology. Key questions to ask for each process step are:

- What could possibly go wrong?

- How likely is it?

- Does it matter – what's the impact?

- Are there any existing mitigations in place (consider TRAM (transfer/reduce/accept/mitigate)) and if so, are they adequate for the level of risk?

To provide clarity when describing risks, the following formula can be used:

X happens because of Y, leading to Z

For example:

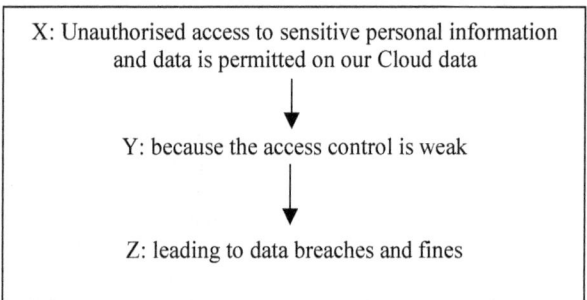

X: Ransomware is installed

↓

Y: due to inadequate training and anti-malware

↓

Z: locking access to our data and systems

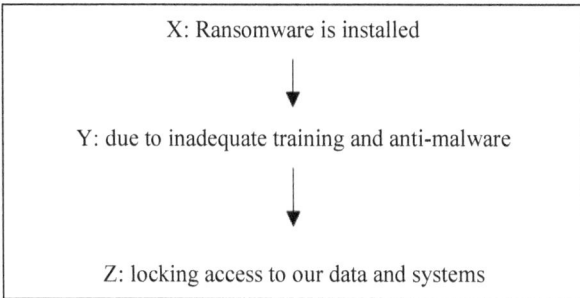

The main way of classifying IT risks is using the initialism CIA (M):

- Confidentiality

- Integrity

- Availability

- Management

These will be explained further in the next chapter.

Where a control is in place, this should be reviewed against the identified risks to consider:

- Is it a detective control to identify an error or attack, where a preventive control would be better?

- If operated properly, would it fully mitigate the risk?

- Is it operated effectively?

- Is it redundant – where, for example, another control already fully mitigates the risk?

The output from this step may be in the form of a risk and controls matrix (RACM). The RACM is a spreadsheet-based document that contains details of the risk and control and can include details such as frequency, location, etc. It should also include details of observed control gaps and weaknesses.

Designing and implementing controls

Objective

Where there are control gaps or inadequacies, new controls will need to be implanted. They should be designed in a way that will mitigate the risk and be easy to operate, ideally automatically operated within the process with minimum impact on its operation.

Often it may not be possible to implement controls immediately, so temporary compensating controls may be required to provide mitigation during this build phase. Accepting the risk by having a 'waiver' (or exception) alone is rarely adequate.

Testing of controls

Where new controls have been designed and implemented, the following testing should be performed:

1. Test design – does the control fully mitigate the risk?

2. Walk-through – has the control been implemented? Is it working as intended?

3. Is evidence retained?

4. Which controls are key?

5. Has all relevant documentation been updated?

6. Are test scripts written in a way that they can be used by others and will generate similar results?

Summary

In this chapter we considered the techniques to identify, assess, build, design, test and monitor controls. In the next chapter we will consider some of the risks and controls specific to cyber.

CHAPTER 4: CYBER RISKS AND CONTROLS

Introduction and overview

The process described in the previous chapter can be used to manage any risk management process, including cyber. Where cyber differs is in the specific nature of the risks faced by organisations and the controls used to mitigate them. Cyber risks can be categorised, like other IT security risks, using CIA.

Confidentiality – relates to organisations' duty of care, and legal responsibility (under the GDPR or other relevant data privacy legislation): they must act as the guardian of the personal and sensitive data they hold on behalf of customers, employees, suppliers, etc. Organisations should also have a means to classify data based on its importance to the business, e.g. information relating to major tenders for new work, or future acquisitions may be regarded as 'most confidential'. Both personal and highly confidential data/related information have value to cyber crooks, terrorists and even nation-state cyber criminals.

Integrity – for example, by changing your data and/or the way it is processed, cyber criminals can fraudulently extract money and cause embarrassment (e.g. inserting inappropriate comments into communications, diverting mail, etc.).

Availability – for example, by locking access to data and systems and/or destroying data backups, crooks can extort money (via ransomware). This can lead to loss of reputation and customers, and additional expense (even if the ransom is not paid).

Organisations should seek to reduce the likelihood that these risks will occur, and their potential business impact if a significant issue arises (including large fines and loss of reputation). There are several frameworks that organisations can use to identify and assess these risks and propose specific controls. One of the most common is the NIST Cybersecurity

Framework, which includes five key functions for cyber activities:

1. **Identify** – know what cyber resources you have and the risks they face.

2. **Protect** – develop, implement and maintain protective safeguards against these risks.

3. **Detect** – be made aware of any unusual or suspicious activity or potential breaches.

4. **Respond** – be able to take appropriate action if a suspected breach occurs.

5. **Recover** – be able to restore activities and provide additional defences for future attacks.

We can use these five functions to review the different risks and controls we would expect to see. There are many tools and applications available to help with each of these control areas.

Identifying cyber risks and controls

Before we can assess protection, we need to understand:

- What assets and information do we have that are at risk?

- What are the cyber risks we face?

- What are the recent changes to specific threats we face?

The assets and information held should be obvious, but often they are not. We live in an age where IT can almost be bought using petty cash, devices on your network may not be owned by your organisation, and asset registers are not updated to reflect changes made, or devices lost or retired. Some cyber risks and controls may be specific to types of device or system (particularly operating systems). Take, for example, the WannaCry attacks on an outdated Microsoft® operating system (XP)[4]. Without knowing what technology you have, appropriate

---

[4] *www.theguardian.com/technology/2017/may/12/nhs-ransomware-cyber-attack-what-is-wanacrypt0r-20*.

controls cannot be developed. Ideally all organisations should have a configuration management database (CMBD). This is a standard requirement for ITIL®, the internationally accepted framework for IT service management (ITSM). As a minimum, organisations should know:

- What cyber security they have;

- How it is identified and where it is;

- The configuration, including the latest patches and anti-malware software;

- How this relates to other assets; and

- What data is held and its sensitivity (level of confidentiality and personal data).

Tools are available to automatically identify changes to configuration. The board should seek evidence that the asst register/CMBD is up to date and has been reviewed.

This can then be used as a basis for forming the risk assessment, and may be a requirement for any cyber insurance cover. It may not be cost effective to cover all risks – but they should at least be considered and reviewed. The risk assessment should also consider the internal and external threats faced both now and in the near future (for example, following the 'go live' of current projects). The process for risk assessment was described in the previous chapter. There should be controls to ensure that the risk assessment has been carried out and is regularly reviewed. This will usually be an annual review and approval.

The threat landscape faced will vary by organisation, its profile and activities. For example, for an oil company there could be increased threats as a result of:

- Large contracts being tendered for – particularly the risk from nation states or large organisations;

- Increased environmental awareness; and

- Media awareness.

These are in addition to the common vulnerabilities found in software, operating systems and hardware.

There is a significant amount of information available in the public domain to make organisations aware of these changing challenges. Many organisations also use a cyber threat monitoring service to keep up to date. These services often have access to additional threat identification resources and can filter threats to assess their likelihood and impact for your specific organisation.

Third-party service providers

Where organisations outsource some or all of their IT or other information-based functions, they are still accountable, and legally responsible for, the CIA of information. For cyber-related services, security needs to be considered at every stage of the third-party lifecycle:

- Supplier selection
- Agreement of contracts
- Duration of contract
- End of service

Cyber criminals may see suppliers as an easy entry into your organisation's cyber defences, hence the need for vigilance throughout the preceding lifecycle.

During the supplier selection process, it is important to ensure that the shortlisted companies can provide a secure and well-managed service, in line with your security expectations. Decisions should not be made based on cost alone. Your organisation should provide its IT security policy and other security compliance requirements to ensure that the shortlisted suppliers are aware of what is expected and confirm that this can be achieved within the service. There should also be some consideration of the provider's ability and willingness to inform your organisation if they suffer a breach.

During the agreement process, you should obtain evidence that the service can be delivered securely – for example from independent (tested) reviews of the supplier's services (e.g. SOC Type 2) and written confirmation of the security requirements. Without these, the supplier may seek additional payment or service variation after the contract has been signed. As part of the agreement, the supplier should be required to:

1. Commit to ongoing compliance for any security requirements;

2. Confirm the monitoring, audit and management reports to be provided, including their frequency, for security management;

3. Confirm that your organisation has a right to access, physically and the service, by penetration testing or other tools;

4. Agree the arrangements for updating the above requirements; and

5. Agree arrangements for securely closing the contract and removing all access to sensitive data.

During the contract, your organisation should ensure that all the promised reports, including audits, are provided and are reviewed. In addition, the right to audit the supplier should be exercised, if available. This helps build the relationship with the supplier and ensures that the service is being provided securely. There are several tools available to help with the assessment of third-party services.

The end of the contract should also be considered so that your organisation can be assured of safe and effective service delivery during the transition and that all data has been handed over or destroyed by the service provider.

The above principles also apply to Cloud-based services. Tools to assist with the risk assessment and review of Cloud-based services are available (e.g. see the Cloud Security Alliance[5]).

Protecting against cyber risks

Having identified the assets and risks/threats, it is then possible to review the controls in place and ensure that they are effective and appropriate. There is a risk of over-control, or having controls in place that do not meet a very high risk or that duplicate another control. In addition to not being cost effective, these could restrict your organisation's ability to make beneficial changes to the way it operates or to enter new markets.

Two models/analogies are often used to describe approaches to cyber protection:

1. The fortress/castle

2. The airport

Consider a castle or fortress and how it is defended: thick walls with small windows, and a moat and drawbridge. Everyone inside is protected to the same level and has the same level of access throughout the fort. The threat is seen as mainly external.

Now consider an airport. Those visiting the airport for a short time (e.g. aircraft enthusiasts, taxi drivers) will be subject to minimal security as they are seen as low risk. Passengers flying will be subject to identity and other security checks, appropriate to the risk of their destination (e.g. lower for domestic flights). Staff and crew will have even more controls, including verification of their identity and access appropriate to their roles, up to flight deck access for flying crew only. Specific access within the complex is based on the need and level of security.

Traditional IT access was based on the fortress model, whereby the same controls were applied to all. This can be expensive to maintain and may leave very important assets at risk, even from internal attack. Many organisations are now moving to a model

---

[5] *https://cloudsecurityalliance.org/.*

like the airport. Data, information and assets are assessed for their sensitivity and importance and then appropriate controls are built. Take, for example, a website – we may want anyone to have access to our 'brochureware', which explains our organisation's background and what we can offer. Access for customers may be restricted by user ID and password so they can check availability and order goods or services. When a customer makes a purchase, we may then have further controls to confirm their identity and check validity of payment. Other areas of the website may be restricted to staff, business partners or loyalty club members. The level of control is related to the level of risk. The same principles may apply not only to access but also to other cyber controls (see Table 2). Both models need to be maintained to ensure integrity of protection.

The two biggest risk areas are where access is inadequate or where there are vulnerabilities within systems. The corresponding controls are summarised in Table 2.

Table 2: Summary of Access Controls

Cyber risk	Common control
Access	• Password and user identification/authorisation • Multi-factor authentication • Firewalls
Vulnerabilities embedded in existing or new software	• Patching • Vulnerability management • Anti-malware • Security by design

Each of these control types is described in the following sections. The additional risk of not identifying or reporting an incident will be considered in the next chapter.

Access management

Poor access management is probably the main risk that is exploited by cyber criminals. This is because it is easy to exploit and it may be difficult to spot where the access appears to be authorised. Access management systems need to be designed, implemented and operated to:

- Confirm the identity of all users, including new users; and

- Ensure users have least privilege – only enough rights to perform their legitimate duties, e.g. to ensure privileged system accounts are only used as authorised and intended.

The processes for access management can be broadly covered as:

- Policy authorisation and implementation;

- Identity management;

- Management of privileged users;

- Access design and implementation; and

- Operation/monitoring.

An authorised policy should define who has access to what, how access is granted or revoked, what actions need to be recorded, and the process for reviewing and updating access rights. Guidance on policy is available in Clause 9 of ISO 27002.

Anyone accessing your systems and data must be properly and immediately identified to ensure they are who they say they are and then be given only their appropriate level of access. The most common way to do this is using a predefined and approved password. Users need to be educated on how to select a password that is not easy to guess; this can be enforced by configuration checks when passwords are created (e.g. ensuring a password includes a mix of upper- and lower-case letters, numbers and special characters, and is not a dictionary-defined word). Where passwords do not provide enough security, multi-factor authentication (based on a code sent to a hardware or software token) or biometrics (based on the physiology of users such as fingerprints) may be required.

Some users will require higher levels of access than others, e.g. being able to manage other users or make system configuration changes. Additional controls to consider are:

- Having separate accounts for when a user is using standard functionality and for when they need privileged access;

- Not allowing access to privileged functions from unsafe devices;

- Requesting independent verification or confirmation such as an additional password when privileged functions are used;

- Requiring evidence for use of the functionality (e.g. ticket details); and

- Monitoring and logging actions taken by privileged accounts and restricting access by location and time of day.

The architectural design of the access management system needs to be secure as this will be a key target for attackers – providing easy access to other functionality.

To support the policy, there should be procedures to monitor and operate access management. For example, arrangements to:

- Reissue forgotten passwords;

- Reopen locked user accounts;

- Enforce password complexity and change;

- Lock or delete obsolete accounts; and

- Review the levels of user access to ensure they are still appropriate.

Firewalls

A firewall acts as a barrier between the networks you trust and those you do not. It provides access control to only trusted networks and filters traffic; some firewalls also provide automatic blocking. They can be software or hardware based or a mixture of the two. Effective firewalls:

- Are installed consistently;

- Are governed by rules appropriate for the level of risk;

- Have rulesets regularly updated and monitored; and

- Are configured according to these rules.

Firewalls may be considered too restrictive where they restrict access for trusted traffic. The danger is changing the rules to be too open (e.g. by allowing an 'any-to-any' rule). Organisations need to consider risk appetite and provide a balance between network accessibility and security.

Security patching

When software suppliers or hardware vendors become aware of bugs within their products, they will issue a patch. This may include solutions for security vulnerabilities or weaknesses. If the software company knows of these vulnerabilities, it is highly likely that cyber criminals will also know and will seek to exploit them (e.g. bypassing access controls to get high-level access privileges). Therefore, it is important to apply patches quickly. Some organisations have a policy of waiting a few weeks to see if any issues arise with the patch (patches are sometimes issued to fix bugs in earlier patches). A better approach is to assess the change based on the information provided and then perform testing of the patch, or a phased rollout to ensure that it does not impact other software in use. For example, some application software may be based on an earlier version of the operating system and so may not work effectively following the update. Where possible, patch updates should be rolled out automatically. Some patches are regularly scheduled (e.g. Microsoft has 'Patch Tuesday' normally on the second Tuesday of each month) or may be emergency patches in response to a sudden threat change.

The effectiveness of patching will depend on having already identified what assets need to be patched. Patching should be a priority and not delayed unless it causes real problems. Patching should be issued and applied automatically centrally within the organisation, and not able to be overridden by user preferences. Where patches cannot be applied, compensating controls should be identified, e.g. the application software causing the conflict could be isolated and replaced.

Vulnerability management

There are several vulnerability management (VM) tools available. Vulnerability management was described by Park Foreman as the "cyclical practice of identifying, classifying, prioritizing, remediating, and mitigating"[6] software vulnerabilities. Vulnerability management tools scan, assess and eliminate known vulnerabilities. Each vulnerability management provider will use publicly available or subscribed sources of vulnerabilities and their own sources. Tools may help identify where, for example, patches have not been applied, and help assess the risk/propose compensating controls. There may also be useful KPIs and other graphical information to summarise the results and impacts for governance and compliance reporting.

Anti-malware

Malware is software intended to do harm to your computers and/or the data they hold. Malware can reduce:

- **Confidentiality** – e.g. by allowing unauthorised access to read or transfer data;

- **Integrity** – e.g. by inserting additional code into programs that leads to fraud; and

---

[6] Park Foreman, *Vulnerability Management*, Taylor & Francis Group, 2010.

- **Availability** – by denying you access, e.g. by installing ransomware to lock your data until a ransom is paid.

Malware takes many forms. The most common are:

- **Viruses/worms** – the malware attaches to another file or program you have legitimately loaded, and often reproduces to infect other programs on the device or network;

- **Trojans** – allow attackers access to infected devices so they can gain higher-level access to data and IT services;

- **Cryptomining** – attackers use your IT resources to perform calculations to mine cryptocurrencies; and

- **Spyware** – covertly watches what is being done and then reports this activity without you knowing (can include smart TVs and other IoT devices).

Cyber criminals and others are constantly seeking to install malware to plant the above on your systems. It is not a question of if there has been an attempt to hack and install malware. It is a question of when – and were you able to stop them.

There are several anti-malware (AM) products available: software that runs in the background (but can also be used to scan files received via email or on media) to scan for known profiles of common malware such as computer viruses. Anti-malware scans, detects and quarantines malware to prevent it becoming embedded in your computers and doing damage. It looks for known fingerprints of malware in expected locations on your computers and enables scans of all files (including email attachments) as required.

Effective anti-malware is:

- Implemented consistently;

- Updated regularly with the latest malware definitions; and

- Used – both in a passive and active mode.

Controls should be in place to ensure that the preceding are being met, and to report instances where anti-malware has not been loaded (installed and operating), scans are not being performed, or definitions are not being updated.

Security by design

The best time to incorporate security into a system or infrastructure is during a major change or development. Adding security later is expensive and may cause unnecessary disruption to the service provided. Cyber services are usually rapidly implemented and there is a risk that security may be overlooked. This can incur additional costs, not only from trying to add security later but also from the loss of business and reputation if insecure software is implemented. Security by design reduces this risk and covers:

- Handling data securely;

- Hardening applications and system settings (e.g. standard secure building of Unix systems); and

- Configuring third-party applications.

Data should be handled securely. For example, particular care should be taken to ensure that data used during development is not based on actual current data files. The system developed should also consider:

- How and where data is to be stored and the period it is to be retained;

- The flow of data through the system and how it will be protected during transit (e.g. use of encryption – with appropriate controls);

- The ability to securely correct corrupted data; and

- Password requirements configured according to risk (e.g. length and complexity of passwords, frequency of change, inactivity time allowed before user is locked out).

Application hardening is a series of technical processes used by developers to reduce the risk that systems will be attacked by improving resistance to unauthorised reverse-engineering or other forms of tampering and intrusion.

The not-for-profit organisation Open Web Application Security Project (OWASP) promotes standards and techniques to:

> make software security visible […] OWASP is in a unique position to provide impartial, practical information about AppSec to individuals, corporations, universities, government agencies, and other organizations worldwide.[7]

Summary

There are several specific areas of risk and control to be considered for cyber. Many of these are based on traditional areas of IT. The key is to consider what the actual risks are and have controls that will mitigate them. These controls should form an effective overall framework to protect the organisation from attack and be able to respond as and when an attack occurs.

---

[7] *www.owasp.org*.

CHAPTER 5: RESPONDING TO AN ATTACK

"If you fail to prepare you are preparing to fail."

Source unknown

Introduction and overview

Even the best controlled organisations are attacked. All organisations must be ready for such an eventuality by planning accordingly and developing processes to detect and respond to an attack.

Preparing for cyber attacks

A key part of preparation is to:

1. Assess which electronic information is vital for the operation of the organisation (sales and staff contact details, key customer details), and ascertain where and how this is stored and can be recovered. Ensure that backup copies of these files are maintained securely and are retrievable (some ransomware attacks seek to destroy backup data before the threat is revealed).

2. Prioritise processes and systems so those with the highest importance can be safeguarded and recovered first if necessary.

3. Consider the reputational impact and how this can be minimised based on different types of cyber incident.

4. If you haven't already, consider the need for cyber insurance, ransomware negotiation support, and access to cyber forensics (to help with evidence gathering and retention) and other specialists.

5. Have an up-to-date plan that is tested and rehearsed based on the most likely high-impact cyber attack or incident.

6. Ensure processes are in place for and key staff are trained in identifying and responding to cyber attacks.

Details of these arrangements should be included in the cyber incident plan.

Detecting potential cyber attacks

Security operations centre

A security operations centre (SOC) is a highly secure location where a team of security engineers monitors and reviews security tools on a 24x7 basis to identify potential attacks (attacks are rarely 9–5, Monday to Friday!). The team uses tools to monitor the IT estate of the organisation to detect any potential attacks and ensure it is ready to react accordingly. Because of the large volumes of data involved, the SOC uses technology or other predefined processes in accordance with the incident plan. A SOC monitors firewalls, servers, PCs, key applications and databases looking for unusual activity. The aim is to shorten the length of time between an attack and its discovery.

Because of the need for highly specialised and trained specialists, several organisations outsource their SOC to a managed security services provider (MSSP). This can have benefits but as with all third-party services, it needs to be properly scoped, selected and implemented. Where non-standard services or reporting are required, this can sometimes incur large costs.

One key tool used by SOCs is security information and event management (SIEM). This is early warning software usually embedded in high-risk servers hosting key applications and databases to look for specific unusual activity based on predefined use cases (e.g. brute-force attack), where many access requests are thrown simultaneously at an application.

Effective SIEM is:

- Properly configured (both for the device and the use cases to be reviewed);

- Monitored, with the output analysed; and

- Maintained to ensure it is updated for any configuration or requirement changes.

IT service helpdesk

IT helpdesk employees should be trained and aware of potential attacks – for example, where there is a sudden increase in calls about:

- Messages demanding a ransom for the release of files;

- PCs, etc. running slower than usual, even after following the normal processes to improve speed;

- Being unable to access accounts or documents;

- Strange emails (one organisation detected an attack because an email claiming to be from the finance department was too polite!);

- Redirected Internet searches going to unusual addresses, e.g. ending in numbers rather than .com; and

- Unexpected account activity (e.g. users seeing that their account was accessed while they were on holiday).

Helpdesks should also be contacted where the SOC suspects an attack (e.g. based on SIEM information).

Recovery following a cyber attack

Once a potential attack has been identified, the cyber incident plan should be initiated. This should include:

Assessing the impact

- Ensuring that evidence of the progress of the attack is recorded and held securely. This will be important for the analysis of the incident to prevent it reoccurring, and may be required for any cyber insurance claim.

- Investigating the nature of the attack, its scope, origin, size, location and the infrastructure impacted.

- Confirming what information may have been breached or changed during the attack.

- Notifying whoever is responsible for resolving the issue and considering who else needs to be informed (regulators, suppliers, customers and insurers).

- Understanding the potential impact on the organisation and ensuring every issue is escalated to the appropriate level of management.

Containing the issue

- Taking appropriate actions, e.g.:

  o Removing and cleaning all infected hardware;

  o Restoring services through backups (if secure);

  o Stopping/removing access used by the perpetrators;

  o Patching all software to the latest level; and

  o Changing passwords for impacted users.

- Reviewing logs to identify other potential targets that may already have been attacked.
- Running anti-malware.
- Checking for unauthorised changes to security software.
- Ensuring communication with the media, etc. is only via pre-agreed channels.
- Issuing warnings to users, regulators and law enforcement as required (e.g. the ICO within 72 hours if a breach of personal data has occurred).

Post-incident

- Reviewing and updating the incident plan based on lessons learned.

- Considering what controls and mitigations need to be strengthened.

Summary

Planning and being able to implement the plan quickly and efficiently should reduce the impact of an attack and ensure that full recovery can be achieved.

CHAPTER 6: CYBER COMPLIANCE

Compliance – noun

"the act or process of complying to a desire, demand, proposal, or regimen […]"

Merriam-Webster Dictionary

Overview and introduction

In the context of cyber we are seeking to comply with our organisation's policies, procedures and processes as well as with legislation. Compliance should not be an annual tick-box exercise, but an opportunity to ensure that controls continue to operate effectively and that the risks of financial penalties and loss of reputation are minimised. It provides assurance that the organisation is taking cyber threats seriously and has controls in place that are designed, implemented and operating effectively. Cyber GRC is not a one-off project, to be completed and then forgotten about. It needs to be embedded as the organisation's usual operations – and a good compliance framework can provide this assurance and identify any areas for continuing improvement, even where there have been changes to requirements, controls or the systems they cover. A good compliance framework should have processes, people and tools that enable a consistent approach over time even where there are other changes.

Compliance also provides assurance to the board, insurers and regulators that proper governance is in place and that cyber controls are working effectively. Having decided what needs to be complied with, a methodology is required to ensure that evidence of compliance can be obtained and provided as required. As it may be the same people responsible or accountable for compliance, regardless of requirement, an approach is needed that can reduce duplication and ensure there are no compliance gaps. There is nothing more frustrating or distracting from the normal day job than to have a series of reviewers/testers asking the same questions. Compliance therefore needs to be a co-ordinated approach to:

1. Identify any major changes;

2. Ensure that controls are still implemented;

3. Ensure that controls are operating as designed and effectively; and

4. Provide evidence.

In this chapter, we will consider the compliance requirements for cyber and provide a framework for achieving cyber compliance.

Cyber compliance requirements

There is no single requirement for cyber compliance. However, there are several existing regulations that do have relevance as shown in Table 3.

Table 3: Cyber Compliance Requirements

Do you …	Applicability (Yes/No)	Requirement
Have an IT security policy?		Comply with own policy
Have ISO 27001 certification (or wish to align with the Standard)?		ISO 27001
Hold and process EU residents' personal data?		GDPR
Provide public essential		Network and Information

services/infrastructure?		Systems (NIS) Regulations
Process card information?		PCI DSS
Have a listing on the US Stock Exchange?		SOX
Obtain IT-related services from third parties?		Third-party compliance – vendor
Provide IT-related services to other organisations?		Third-party compliance – supplier
Have a cyber insurance policy?		Cyber insurance policy clauses
Have a cyber certification (e.g. Cyber Essentials)?		Compliance with the scheme's requirements

These are intended for guidance only, as each organisation needs to assess its cyber compliance requirements. Also be aware that this is a very dynamic area, so the requirements and the locations of operation are changing over time. Even where there is no obligation to comply, the principles of these requirements may be applied to provide greater assurance to organisations that they have sound cyber security defences. Next is a brief summary of each requirement, its applicability and key features.

IT (or information) security policy

All organisations should have an IT security policy to identify their requirements to users, vendors and other interested stakeholders, and to set the agreed parameters for cyber security. Often these will be aligned with international standards such as ISO 27001. Such alignment can assist when comparing policies for different organisations (e.g. following the acquisition of a company, reviewing the alignment of the policies for the two entities). The use of ISO 27001 referencing can greatly assist with this process. The policy should be reviewed, updated and communicated on a regular basis. It may also be supported by other Standards such as acceptable use of IT.

The policy should clearly identify those requirements that are mandatory ('must') and those that are preferred ('should'). It may indicate where special attention needs to be applied, e.g. for systems processing 'Most Confidential' (i.e. restricted access – for example, relating to potential mergers and acquisitions), or personal data.

Policy content may vary but generally will include cyber security requirements for:

- Compliance requirements;
- System development and change;
- Access and authorisation;
- Network security;
- Third parties;
- Anti-malware;
- IT and security operations;
- Business continuity; and
- Wireless security.

It is also useful to map each of the policy statements under the preceding headings to the other compliance requirements as identified in the introduction. This eases the complaints process and helps confirm the policy's completeness and breadth of coverage.

Some policies also include suggested controls. In checking compliance needs to ensure compliance with the actual policy statement, any described controls should be illustrative only and not a specific compliance requirement. If the requirement is fully met, and the approach clearly defined, this should be sufficient.

ISO 27001

ISO (International Organization for Standardization) provides globally recognised and adopted standards. These are written, reviewed and approved under tight controls. The ISO/IEC 27000 group of standards focuses on the security of information assets. The main standard in this group for cyber security is ISO 27001, which provides "requirements for establishing, implementing, maintaining and continually improving an information security management system [ISMS]."[8]

An ISMS is a system of people, processes and IT systems, with a risk assessment at its core, and is applicable regardless of organisation size. Each organisation should apply the Standard based on its needs and objectives, security requirements, the organisational processes used, and its size and structure. The Standard uses CIA introduced earlier in this book. The adoption of the Standard provides assurance that a risk management process has been applied and that IT security risks (including cyber) are managed effectively. It can also be used as a basis for reviewing compliance with the organisation's own requirements (e.g. as stated in the IT security policy).

There are several services available to implement ISO 27001 or to provide an independent audit of compliance.

General Data Protection Regulation (GDPR)

The protection of personal data and how it is used has been regulated since 1982. The latest legislation is the GDPR, which includes several rights for EU residents (data subjects) to ensure that their data is used safely and as intended. These rights could be considered responsibilities for organisations processing personal data and hence areas where they need to ensure that they comply with GDPR. Data subjects must:

- Be informed if their personal data is being used; and
- Be able to:

---

[8] *www.iso.org/isoiec-27001-information-security.html*.

- o Obtain copies of their data;

- o Enquire as to the use or storage of their personal data;

- o Have data errors corrected;

- o Challenge data accuracy;

- o Request deletion of data;

- o Limit the way an organisation uses their personal data;

- o Get their personal data from an organisation in a way that is accessible; and

- o Object to the use of their data under some circumstances.

Data subjects also have rights relating to decisions made based on automated processing.

These rights are far reaching, and personal data breaches can lead to substantial fines for the organisation. For cyber compliance, organisations need to:

- Map and locate personal data they hold;

- Ensure data is held securely (even if it is in the Cloud or with third parties);

- Conduct a data protection impact assessment (DPIA) for any planned major changes or developments;

- Have processes in place to respond effectively to data subject requests and enquiries;

- Ensure they comply with the above principles; and

- Have processes in place to notify the ICO (within 72 hours) if a breach occurs.

Network and Information Systems (NIS) requirements

The EU's Directive on security of network and information systems (NIS Directive), adopted in 2016, and enacted in UK law as The Network and Information Systems Regulations (NIS Regulations) in May 2018,[9] seeks to ensure that security, including cyber security, for infrastructure of national importance and criticality is resilient to any attacks. There are three parts:

1. **National capabilities** – EU member states must have national cyber security capabilities (in the UK, the National Centre for Cyber Security (NCSC)).

2. **Cross-border collaboration** – encourages cross-border collaboration and information sharing to reduce the risk of attack and improve responsiveness.

3. **National supervision of critical sectors** – covers areas such as energy, transport, water, health and the finance sector.

There are no specific compliance requirements, but the sharing of information can provide a useful source of checks to be included in compliance. Within the UK, the NCSC has set specific objectives and principles with mandatory security outcomes for those organisations providing critical services:

a) **Managing security risk** – governance, risk management, asset management and supply chain.

b) **Protecting against cyber attack** – policies and process, identity and access control, data security, system security, resilience of networks and systems, staff awareness and training.

c) **Detecting cyber security events** – security monitoring, anomaly detection.

---

[9] *www.itgovernancepublishing.co.uk/product/network-and-information-systems-nis-regulations-a-pocket-guide-for-operators-of-essential-services.*

d) **Minimising the impact of cyber security incidents –** response and recovery planning, lessons learned.

Payment Card Industry Data Security Standard

The Payment Card Industry Data Security Standard (PCI DSS) is a set of security requirements for the secure processing of card details, and applies to any organisation that accepts, processes, transmits or stores card details. Compliance levels are determined by individual payment brands or acquiring banks, based on individual payment brands. Compliance is based on specified controls and on a three-step process:

1. Assessing – knowing what cardholder data is held, listing payment card processing IT assets and business processes, and assessing for vulnerabilities. Assessments are performed by Qualified Security Assessors – individuals who work for companies qualified by the PCI Security Standards Council to perform these assessments.

2. Remediating these vulnerabilities and ensuring cardholder data is only stored if absolutely necessary.

3. Reporting – submitting required reports to the appropriate acquiring bank/card brand.

Sarbanes-Oxley Act

The US Sarbanes-Oxley Act was introduced in 2002 in response to a loss of faith in financial reporting for US registered companies (e.g. Enron).[10] For cyber compliance there are two elements:

1. Cyber security reporting of risk management and incidents throughout the year.

2. General IT controls that include cyber elements – e.g. access controls, incident management.

10

https://corporatefinanceinstitute.com/resources/knowledge/other/enron-scandal/.

Controls are designed, implemented and operated by the organisation where the risk would impact the accuracy of financial reporting. Organisations listed in the US should ensure compliance and the controls are subject to annual audit by external auditors. Failure to comply or be audited can result in civil and criminal actions, including against directors.

Third-party compliance

The responsibility for operating cyber controls can be partly delegated to a service provider, but still needs to be controlled. Accountability, including the need for legal compliance, cannot be delegated. A customer organisation therefore still needs to ensure compliance. The compliance requirements should be detailed in the initial contract – otherwise additional costs or risks may be incurred. Compliance should include:

1. Ensuring key performance and management indicators for security services and processes are received and reviewed on a regular basis;

2. Updating the provider on any changes impacting the service;

3. Notifying the customer promptly of any changes to controls at the provider, or any known breaches or incidents; and

4. Ensuring independent auditors' reports are received and reviewed for relevance and the right to audit is exercised if required.

Where the organisation is a service provider, the converse of the above will apply.

Cyber insurance policy clauses

Organisations should review their level of cover and need for cyber insurance. These policies can reduce the impact and cost of an attack, including third-party claims. This allows for the use of technical and other support. However, like all insurance policies, they may include exclusion clauses. It is therefore important for organisations to ensure compliance with these requirements in order not to lose cover. In addition to the normal information required for any type of policy, organisations may be required to provide details of data types and volumes; employment of IT, information and cyber security specialists; existing security arrangements; and history of any cyber incidents.

The policies can be highly tailored, and exclusions and conditions can vary significantly between providers. To ensure compliance, the insured organisation needs to:

1. Ensure that the information provided on the application is up to date and still accurate;

2. Ensure correct claim processes, including timing of notification and by whom, are adhered to; and

3. Obtain prior consent from the insurer before incurring costs as a result of the incident and ensure that the professionals selected meet the criteria of the insurer.

Summary

To be cyber compliant, organisations need effective and up-to-date IT security policies and related procedures. These should be implemented and communicated so that compliance can be monitored and reviewed to identify areas of potential weakness and attack. In addition, there may be specific compliance requirements, based on the sector of operations and range of activities.

BOOKS BY THE SAME AUTHOR

- *Agile Governance and Audit – An overview for auditors and agile teams* (published by ITGP, 2014) www.itgovernancepublishing.co.uk/product/agile-governance-and-audit

- *Fundamentals of Assurance for Lean Projects – An overview for auditors and project teams* (published by ITGP, 2017) www.itgovernancepublishing.co.uk/product/fundamentals-of-assurance-for-lean-projects

- *Fundamentals of Information Security Risk Management Auditing – An introduction for managers and auditors* (published by ITGP, 2016), www.itgovernancepublishing.co.uk/product/fundamentals-of-information-security-risk-management-auditing

- *Reviewing IT in Due Diligence – Are you buying an IT asset or liability?* Co-written with Bryan Altimas (published by ITGP, 2015), www.itgovernancepublishing.co.uk/product/reviewing-it-in-due-diligence

FURTHER READING

IT Governance Publishing (ITGP) is the world's leading publisher for governance and compliance. Our industry-leading pocket guides, books, training resources and toolkits are written by real-world practitioners and thought leaders. They are used globally by audiences of all levels, from students to C-suite executives.

Our high-quality publications cover all IT governance, risk and compliance frameworks and are available in a range of formats. This ensures our customers can access the information they need in the way they need it.

Our other publications about cyber security include:

- *The Tao of Open Source Intelligence* by Stewart Bertram, *www.itgovernancepublishing.co.uk/product/the-tao-of-open-source-intelligence*

- *Cyberwar, Cyberterror, Cybercrime & Cyberactivism – An in-depth guide to the role of standards in the cybersecurity environment, Second edition* by Julie Mehan, *www.itgovernancepublishing.co.uk/product/cyberwar-cyberterror-cybercrime-cyberactivism-2nd-edition*

- *Build a Security Culture* by Kai Roer, *www.itgovernancepublishing.co.uk/product/build-a-security-culture*

For more information on ITGP and branded publishing services, and to view our full list of publications, visit *www.itgovernancepublishing.co.uk*.

To receive regular updates from ITGP, including information on new publications in your area(s) of interest, sign up for our newsletter at www.itgovernancepublishing.co.uk/topic/newsletter.

Branded publishing

Through our branded publishing service, you can customise ITGP publications with your company's branding.

Find out more at
www.itgovernancepublishing.co.uk/topic/branded-publishing-services.

Related services

ITGP is part of GRC International Group, which offers a comprehensive range of complementary products and services to help organisations meet their objectives.

For a full range of resources on cyber security visit www.itgovernance.co.uk/shop/category/cyber-security.

Training services

The IT Governance training programme is built on our extensive practical experience designing and implementing management systems based on ISO standards, best practice and regulations.

Our courses help attendees develop practical skills and comply with contractual and regulatory requirements. They also support career development via recognised qualifications.

Learn more about our training courses in cyber security and view the full course catalogue at www.itgovernance.co.uk/training.

Professional services and consultancy

We are a leading global consultancy of IT governance, risk management and compliance solutions. We advise businesses around the world on their most critical issues and present cost-saving and risk-reducing solutions based on international best practice and frameworks.

We offer a wide range of delivery methods to suit all budgets, timescales and preferred project approaches.

Further reading

Find out how our consultancy services can help your organisation at *www.itgovernance.co.uk/consulting*.

Industry news

Want to stay up to date with the latest developments and resources in the IT governance and compliance market? Subscribe to our Weekly Round-up newsletter and we will send you mobile-friendly emails with fresh news and features about your preferred areas of interest, as well as unmissable offers and free resources to help you successfully start your projects. *www.itgovernance.co.uk/weekly-round-up*.

EU for product safety is Stephen Evans, The Mill Enterprise Hub, Stagreenan, Drogheda, Co. Louth, A92 CD3D, Ireland. (servicecentre@itgovernance.eu)

www.ingramcontent.com/pod-product-compliance
Lightning Source LLC
Chambersburg PA
CBHW071120210326
41519CB00020B/6362